Body Talk

Move Your Body

BONES AND MUSCLES

Steve Parker

www.raintreepublishers.co.uk
Visit our website to find out more information about **Raintree** books.

To order:
☎ Phone 44 (0) 1865 888113
📄 Send a fax to 44 (0) 1865 314091
💻 Visit the Raintree bookshop at **www.raintreepublishers.co.uk**
to browse our catalogue and order online.

First published in Great Britain by Raintree,
Halley Court, Jordan Hill, Oxford, OX2 8EJ,
part of Harcourt Education.
Raintree is a registered trademark of Harcourt
Education Ltd.

© Harcourt Education Ltd 2006
The moral right of the proprietor has been
asserted.

Editorial: Melanie Waldron, Rosie Gordon,
and Megan Cotugno
Design: Philippa Jenkins, Lucy Owen,
and John Walker
Illustrations: Darren Linguard, Jeff Edwards
Picture Research: Mica Brancic and
Ginny Stroud-Lewis
Production: Chloe Bloom

Originated by Dot Gradations Ltd, UK
Printed and bound in China by South China
Printing Company

10 digit ISBN: 1 406 20064 6
13 digit ISBN: 978 1 4062 0064 5
10 09 08 07 06
10 9 8 7 6 5 4 3 2 1

**British Library Cataloguing in
Publication Data**
Parker, Steve
  Move your body! : bones and muscles. - (Body
talk)
  1.Bones - Juvenile literature 2.Muscles -
Juvenile literature
I.Title
  612.7
A full catalogue record for this book is available
from the British Library.

Acknowledgements
The publishers would like to thank the following
for permission to reproduce photographs:
Alamy Images pp. 24-25 (Aflo Foto Agency), pp.
4-5 (Buzz Pictures), pp. 28-29 (UKraft); Corbis
pp. 12-13, 14-15, 16-17, 24-25, 26-27, 32-33,
36-37, 38-39 (Anders Ryman), pp. 26-27 (Arko
Datta/Reuters), pp. 40-41 (Cheque), pp. 20-21,
34-35 (Duomo), pp. 10-11 (Eric Gaillard/
Reuters), pp. 36-37 (Herb Swanson/ Reuters), pp.
36-37L (Michael Wong), pp. 34-35 (Roy
Morsch), pp. 14-15 (Tracy Kahn); Getty Images
pp. 6-7; 18-19, 30-31 (Allsport Concepts), pp.
10-11 (PhotoDisc), 32-33 (Photographers'
Choice), pp. 10-11, 30-31, 34-35 (The Image
Bank); Harcourt Education Ltd/Tudor
Photography pp. 12-13; Science Photo Library
pp. 18-19, 42-43; 16-17 (Andrew Leonard), pp.
8-9 (Andrew Syred/MANFRED KAGE), pp. 14-15
(BSIP Dr T Pichard), pp. 20-21 (Chris Bjornberg),
pp. 28-29 (Clara Franzini Armstrong), pp. 42-43
(Damien Lovegrove), pp. 18-19 (Dave Roberts),
pp. 22-23 (David Gifford), p. 24 (Dept. Of
Clinical Radiology, Salisbury District Hospital),
pp. 20-21 (Mehau Kulyk), pp. 6-7 (Pasieka), pp.
26-27 (Sheila Terry). Cover photograph of man
in dance pose reproduced with permission of
Getty Images/Stone/Ryan McVay.

The author and publisher would like to thank
Ann Fullick for her assistance in the preparation
of this book.

Dedicated to the memory of Lucy Owen

Contents

Any words appearing in the text in bold, **like this**, are explained in the glossary. You can also look out for them in 'Body language' at the bottom of each page.

Get a move on!

Are you moving? You may not look like it, as you sit quietly and read. But you are breathing (hopefully!)... Also, your heart is beating inside your chest. Your gut muscles are squeezing food along. The inside of your body is never perfectly still. This is because of the muscles that are working all the time to keep you alive.

On the go

When you turn this page, scratch your ear, or leap up, more muscles are at work. These muscles pull on your bones to make your whole body move.

Your bones are not just there to hold you up and stop you flopping on the floor as a soggy heap. They are pulled by your muscles, to make you walk, run, jump, lift, bend, kick, push, bite, and chew.

"When I did my first somersault, I was so happy that I almost fell off."

Katie, under-16 years champion gymnast, talking about when she was practising on the narrow beam at the age of 11.

Push on the pedals, lean back, ➤ turn the handlebars, tilt the body, bend the neck slightly, twist the wrist – all these tiny movements merge into an amazing mid air trick. And they're all made by muscles pulling bones.

Working together

So, your bones give you a firm framework, and your muscles give you the power to move. But there is another body part that you can't move without – the brain.

Your brain controls your muscles and actions. It learns to make new, skilful movements and easily carries out older ones. When you have finished this sentence, try one of them – turn the page.

them – turn the page.

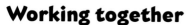

Find out later ...

Why is your nose so squashy?

How many muscles does a body builder have?

How complicated is throwing a ball?

No bag of bones!

You are certainly not a "bag of bones"! But about one–seventh of your body weight is bones – you have more than 200 of them. Together they form your skeleton. This is your inner support and framework.

A skeleton works like the steel beams inside a skyscraper. It holds you up so you can stand straight and tall. Without a skeleton, you would be as floppy and helpless as a jellyfish stranded on the beach.

Inside out?

We have our skeletons on the inside. So do other creatures like dogs, cats, birds, snakes and fish. But other animals have a skeleton on the outside, as a hard body covering. Crabs, snails, and insects like beetles have this design. A skeleton on the outside is called an exoskeleton.

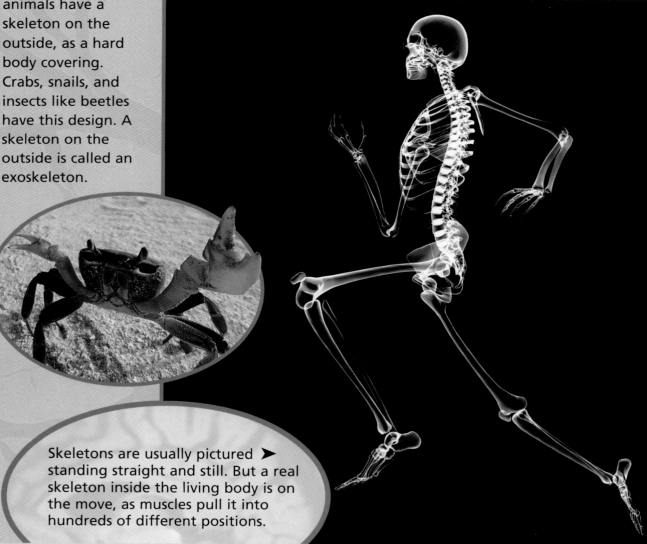

Skeletons are usually pictured ➤ standing straight and still. But a real skeleton inside the living body is on the move, as muscles pull it into hundreds of different positions.

cartilage   tough, springy substance, sometimes called "gristle", that covers the end of bones inside a joint, and forms some parts of the skeleton

Skeleton from top to toes

At the top of the skeleton is your **skull**. It forms a hard case around your brain for protection, and gives shape to your face.

Below your skull is your body's main central support column – your backbone or spine. On each side of the upper backbone are your shoulder and arm bones. At the bottom of your backbone is the wide hip bone, and linked to this are your leg bones.

So many shapes

Each bone has a special shape, to do its task as part of the whole skeleton. Your arm and leg bones are long and slim. They work like **levers** so you can reach out, lift and push with your arms, and walk, run and kick with your legs.

The bones in your shoulders and hips are broad and flattened. They have large surfaces where the powerful muscles needed to move your arms and legs are attached.

When "bone" is not bone

Not all parts of the skeleton are made of bone. Some parts are made of a lighter, slightly softer, bendier substance called **cartilage** or "gristle". The front of each rib, where it joins the breastbone, is made of cartilage.

BONE RECORDS

- Total number of bones in an adult man or woman: 206.
- Longest bone: thigh bone (femur), which forms one-quarter of your total body height.
- Widest bone: hip bone (pelvis), which is the broadest part of the body.
- Smallest bone: stirrup bone (stapes) deep in the ear, which is the shape of this letter "U", and just 8mm high.
- Strongest bone for its size: lower jaw (mandible).

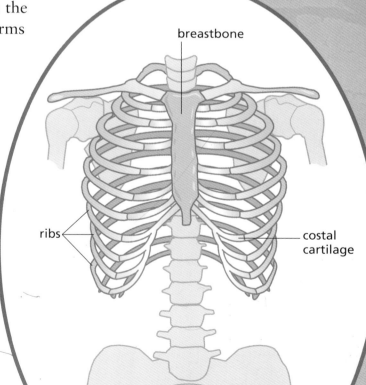

breastbone

ribs

costal cartilage

skull main bone inside the head, which is really more than 20 bones joined together
lever crowbar-like, able to move heavy loads

How strong is bone?

Bone is amazingly strong, yet light too. If your skeleton was made of steel, it would weigh five times more. A skeleton of aluminium, wood or plastic might be as light as bone, but not as strong. And bone beats all of these in another way – it can mend itself.

Bones alive!

Maybe you've seen old bones, on display in a museum or exhibition, or perhaps animal bones out in the countryside. They look dry, brittle and cracked. But inside the body, living bones are very different. They are not dead and cracked, but very much alive. They are tough and slightly bendy.

Like other body parts, bones have **blood vessels** to bring them **nutrients**, and nerves to feel if they are being pressed or bent.

Look at the inside of a bone ➤ under a powerful microscope and this is what you see. The dark area is a "Haversian canal", with miniature blood vessels and nerves at its centre (shown in red).

blood vessel   arteries, capillaries, and veins, through which blood flows
bone marrow   jelly-like substance inside certain bones, which makes new blood cells and stores nutrients

Micro-bone

The body is made of billions of tiny "building blocks" called **cells**. Bones contain cells too. But they don't have as many cells as most other body parts. This is because parts of a bone are made of two other substances. One is **collagen**, which is also found in the skin. It looks like tiny strings or fibres. The other is tiny crystals of minerals, especially calcium and phosphate.

A bone contains millions of these fibres and crystals. They are made by bone cells, which keep them in top condition, so the bone stays strong and healthy.

Inside a bone

Most bones have three layers, one inside the other. On the outside is very strong, solid material called compact bone. The middle layer is like hard sponge and is called spongy bone. In the middle is soft, jelly-like **bone marrow**.

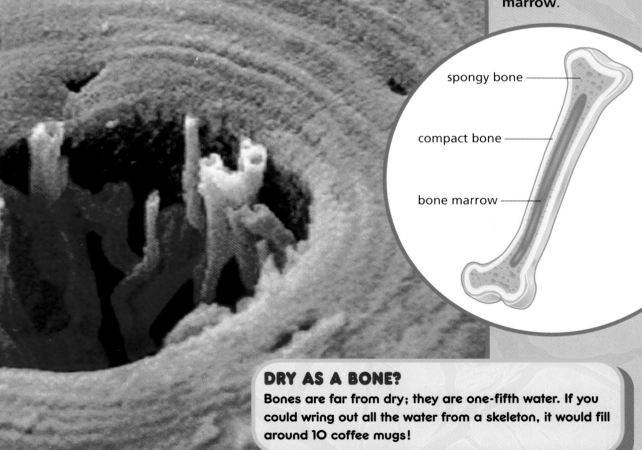

spongy bone

compact bone

bone marrow

DRY AS A BONE?

Bones are far from dry; they are one-fifth water. If you could wring out all the water from a skeleton, it would fill around 10 coffee mugs!

collagen   tough, string-like fibres in certain body parts such as skin and bones
nutrients   substances in food that the body needs to be healthy, grow and heal

Where's your nose?

When we see pictures of skulls, they have no noses – and no ears either! Why? Because the nose and ears are not made of hard, long-lasting bone. They are made of softer, bendier **cartilage**. After death, this does not last nearly so long as bone.

Bone head!

Tap the top of your head gently. It feels hard and sounds strong (and hopefully not hollow!). Just under your hair and skin is the main bone inside your head, your **skull**. In fact, the skull is not one single bone. It is made of 21 bones joined together very tightly and firmly, plus one bone that can move. Eight of the fixed-together skull bones form a dome shape, like an upside-down bowl. This is called the **cranium** or "brain-box". It wraps around your brain and protects it from bangs and knocks.

QUICK QUIZ
Can you match these bone names with the letters on the skull drawing?

Lacrimal bone

Nasal bone

Frontal bone

Temporal bone

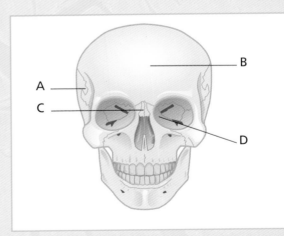

Here are some clues: Your temples are the sides of your head, just above your ears. 'Lacrimal' is to do with crying. Answers are on page 44.

In your face!

The other 13 fixed-together skull bones are inside your face. If you touch gently just below your eye, you can feel one of them – the cheek bone. In fact, around each of your eyes there are six curved bones. Like the bones around your brain, these face bones form a bowl shape around your eye, called the eye socket. This protects the eye from damage.

So which is the only part of your skull that can move? Open your mouth to answer, and this is it – your lower jaw. It moves at the jaw joints, just below your ears, as you eat and talk.

▼ After someone dies, the body parts that last longest are bones – especially the skull. For many years the skull has been used as a sign of danger and death.

I recognise you!

Your skull helps to make you – you! The bones of your skull give your face and head their shape, so people recognize you. Look at your family and friends. Notice how their faces vary – wide or narrow, large forehead or small chin. These shapes are mainly due to the skull bones.

The cushions in the spine

Between each pair of bones in the backbone, there is a disc of **cartilage**, like a strong cushion. This is called an intervertebral disc. It holds the bones apart slightly and lets them tilt. Sometimes this disc gets squeezed too much, pokes out, presses on a nerve and causes pain. This is a "slipped disc".

Stand up straight!

One second you can stand up tall and straight, the next you can bend down almost double, and perhaps even touch your toes with your fingers. This is due to your bendy backbone, also called your spine. The spine forms almost half of the body's height. It is strong enough to hold up the head, arms and upper body. But it is not one bone. It is 26 separate bones, one on top of the other. These bones are called **vertebrae**. They are joined like links in a chain. Each one can move only a little against those above and below it. But over the whole backbone, these many little movements add up to a lot.

> With proper teaching and practice, ➤ some people can bend their backs more than normal. The backbone curves so much that it forms not just a U-shape, but a C- or even an O-shape.

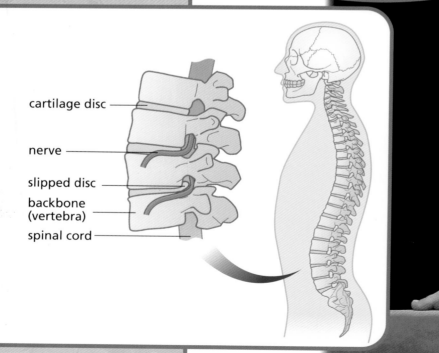

cartilage disc

nerve

slipped disc

backbone (vertebra)

spinal cord

nerves   string-like parts that carry messages around the body as tiny pulses of electricity

What a nerve!

The backbone is not solid, like a rod. It is hollow, like a bendy tube. Inside it is your **spinal cord** – your main **nerve**. It connects your brain, in the **skull** on top of the backbone, with all the other parts of your body. It carries messages to your brain, about what you touch and feel with your skin. It carries messages from your brain to your muscles, telling them when to move. The spinal cord is very delicate and precious. But it is well protected from being squeezed and knocked, inside the backbone.

"I've done my back in"

Many people suffer from backache at some time in life. Often this is due to lifting and twisting at the same time. It's useful to know about lifting heavy objects properly, to avoid back strain.

Lift heavy items by bending your knees instead of your back.

spinal cord   main nerve linking the brain to the rest of the body
vertebrae   individual bones of the spinal column, which join like links in a chain

More jobs for bones

Your bones don't just hold you up and let you move about. They also protect your soft inside parts. The dome of your **skull** covers and protects your most precious body part – your brain. Also, just inside this dome there are three soft, bag-like layers known as **meninges**, plus a layer of liquid too. The meninges and liquid wrap around and cover the brain. They form a soft cushion between the skull and the brain, for even better protection when the head is knocked or hit.

Extra help

The skull bone around the brain is very strong. But a hard knock could break it, and badly damage the brain. People at risk of head injury wear helmets or hard-hats. They include cyclists, motorcyclists, canoeists, climbers, cavers, workers in factories and on building sites ... and many more.

meninges   three thin layers that protect and nourish the brain and spinal cord

Inside a cage

Your heart beats and your lungs fill with air – and bones protect them. The backbone at the rear, the curved ribs around the side, and the breastbone at the front, all make up your chest. They form a "cage" around the heart and lungs to shield them from knocks and damage. What's more, this cage can move. Your ribs tilt up and out every time you breathe. This allows your lungs to get bigger and suck in air for breathing.

"On the way down my snowboard hit a rock and threw me sideways into a tree. I banged by head really hard – thankfully I was wearing my helmet."

Ed, after his first big snowboarding fall.

◄ Soccer players are taught to head the ball correctly using the forehead. The delicate brain is just beneath, and could be shaken and damaged by heading the ball wrongly.

Small shield

The kneecap is a small bone that works as a protector. It is like a little shield that guards the knee joint just behind it. Next time you knock or graze your knee, remember that your kneecap has done its job well.

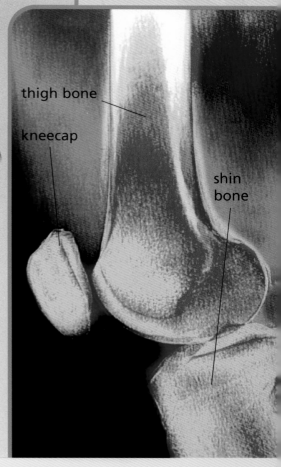

thigh bone

kneecap

shin bone

Busy bones

Your bones are not simply solid supports that hold you up and protect your soft inside parts. They are very, very busy! One of their extra tasks is making new blood.

Your blood contains red **blood** cells to carry life-giving **oxygen** around your body, and white blood cells to fight germs. Every minute, as part of normal body wear and tear, millions of these blood cells die. But your bones make new ones to replace them. These blood cells are made in the soft, jelly-like **marrow** found inside most bones. The marrow makes lots – three million new blood cells every second!

Narrow marrow

Bone marrow is in the narrow centre of most bones. Here, microscopic marrow stem cells are busy multiplying. Each cell splits in half and the halves grow into full cells, again and again, every few hours. The extra cells they make gradually change shape and become new blood cells, like the white blood cells below.

BONE MINERALS

These minerals are found mainly in the bones. But they are used for other body processes too.

- **Calcium:** The body contains about 1,200 grams and 99 per cent is in the bones and teeth.
- **Phosphorus:** The body contains over 500 grams, and 86 per cent is in the bones and teeth.
- **Magnesium:** The body contains about 25 grams, and 60 per cent is in the bones and teeth.

oxygen   gas, which makes up one-fifth of air, that each body cell needs
minerals   substances, such as iron, that the body needs to stay healthy

Stores

Bones also store important body **minerals**. You need minerals like iron and **calcium** in your food to keep your body working well. But some people may not have enough healthy food for a while. So minerals are sent from their bone stores to the body parts where they are needed more urgently.

For example, calcium is needed for strong bones – but also for sending nerve messages. If there isn't enough calcium in food, calcium supplies may pass from bones to **nerves**, so the nerves can work. Later, when there is enough healthy food, the bones take in their calcium again.

Bigger bones

It is not hard to get healthy, tough bones. Food and drink rich in calcium, like milk, can help you prevent bone injuries in the future. Children and babies need the most calcium because their bones are still growing.

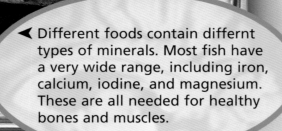

◄ Different foods contain differnt types of minerals. Most fish have a very wide range, including iron, calcium, iodine, and magnesium. These are all needed for healthy bones and muscles.

One-sided sports

In many sports, one arm and hand are used much more than the other. So this arm usually has stronger muscles and slightly larger, tougher bones, compared to the other.

Growing bones

When you were born you had about 350 bones – but as an adult, you will only have 206. What's going on?

This happens because of the way bones form when an unborn baby is very tiny, smaller than a thumb. At this stage, many of your "bones" were made of the slightly softer, gristly substance called **cartilage**. Gradually, as you grew from a newborn baby into a child, some of these small, soft cartilage bones **fused** together strongly, forming fewer, larger bones.

Slowly, over the years, the cartilage shapes turn into real bone. By about 20 years of age, your skeleton will be fully-grown and nearly all bone.

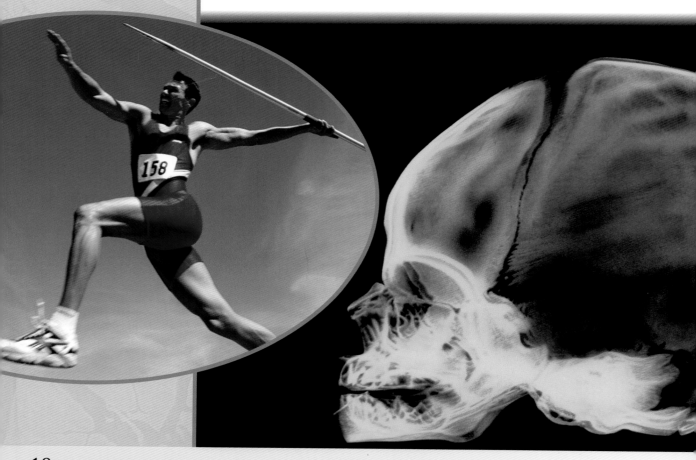

fontanelle   gaps between the skull bones of a baby, which eventually close
fracture   break or crack

Changing and mending

Did you know that bones do not stay exactly the same shape? If your body repeats the same movements often, like lifting a weight, then your muscles get bigger and stronger, and so do your bones.

If you are right-handed, the bones and muscles are probably slightly bigger and stronger in your right arm and hand, compared to your left. Can you see any difference?

Bones can mend themselves if they fracture. This happens more quickly when we are young, because the bones are still growing. As we get older, bones break more easily and also take longer to repair themselves.

Put back together

Even badly broken bones can mend themselves. But doctors make sure that the broken parts are put back together as perfectly as possible. Otherwise the bone takes longer to heal, and even when it does, it may be out of shape and not very strong.

DID YOU KNOW?

Feel your hard "ankle" bones, on the inside and outside of your lower leg. But these are not really ankle bones at all. They are the sticking-out ends of the long bones in your shin. The real ankle bones are below them, in front of your heel.

◄ In a baby's skull, some of the bones are separate and not yet joined together. Between them are gaps called **fontanelles**. (Compare this baby's skull with the adult one on page 21.) This allows the baby's skull to be squashed as it is born without any damage to the baby or the mum.

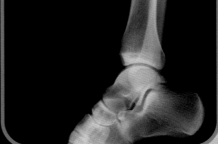

fuse   join very strongly, so hardly any joint remains

Flexi-body

Your skeleton is strong and tough, and gives you support and protection. But you wouldn't move an inch if you had no joints.

A joint is where two or more bones are linked together. Your body has more than 200 joints. Most let you bend or straighten parts of your body when your muscles pull on the bones.

New joints for old

In some people, joints become stiff and painful, especially after many years of hard use. Doctors can carry out an operation to remove the old, worn parts of the joint, and put in a new one made of metal and plastic, called an artificial joint. This can be done in the hip, knee, elbow and even the finger knuckles.

As the baseball player pitches ➤ the ball, her shoulder, elbow, wrist and finger joints change the shape of her arm, from bent behind her shoulder, to straight out in front of her.

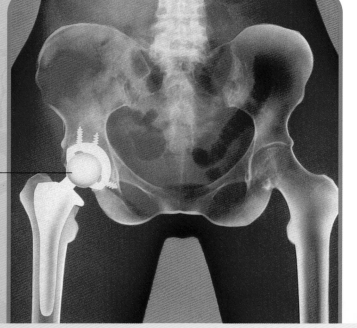

artificial hip joint ——

sprain   when a joint is forced to move too far, damaging the soft parts
sutures   fixed joints, where bones have joined solidly together

Bendy – but not that bendy

Have you ever "twisted" your ankle? Or bent your fingers back, for example, when trying to catch a fast-moving ball? If this causes a lot of pain, it could be a **sprained** joint. A sprain happens because most of the body's joints are limited in their movement. The bones can only move a certain amount and no further. In a sprain, the bones are forced too far and stretch the soft parts inside the joint, causing damage, swelling and pain.

Joints with no point?

Some of your joints cannot move at all! The bones are fixed together firmly and the joint does not bend. The main examples are the joints between the separate bones of your skull and the bones that make up your pelvis, or hip bone. The only signs of these joints are wiggly lines called **sutures**, where the bones meet. In the skull, these bones were separate when you were born (see pages 18-19).

sutures

Inside a joint

The oily fluid inside a joint is made by the inside lining of the joint capsule. Even in big joints like the hip and knee, only about a teaspoon of fluid is needed.

Smooth moves

Bend and straighten your wrist and fingers, and listen to them carefully. Can you hear any creaking or scraping noises? Hopefully not – your movements are silent. The body's joints work very smoothly and quietly, because of the way they are made.

First, where the bones meet inside a joint, each has a covering of **cartilage**. This is smooth, shiny, slippery and slightly soft. Bare bones would rub and scrape each other as the joint moved. But with their cartilage coverings, they slip easily past each other.

The knee is an unusual joint. As well as cartilage covering the ends of the bones, it has two curved extra pieces of cartilage between the bones for extra protection. These can be squashed or cracked by sudden twisting movements. The damage is "torn knee cartilage". ▼

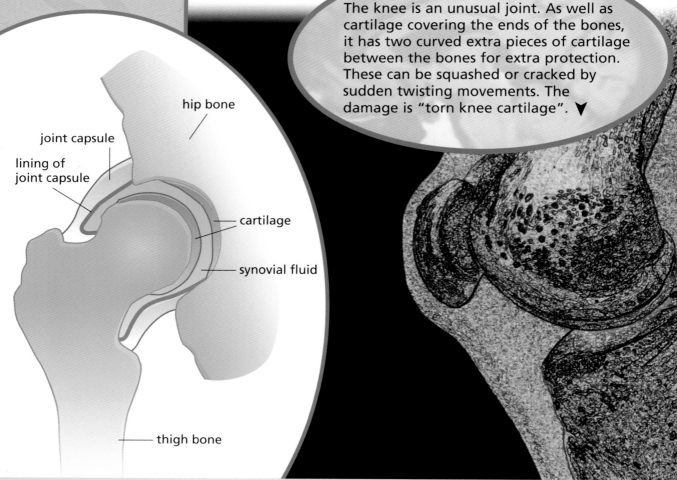

hip bone

joint capsule

lining of joint capsule

cartilage

synovial fluid

thigh bone

joint capsule bag-like part around the bone ends in a joint, containing synovial fluid
ligament "strap" that holds bones at a joint and stops them moving too far

Oil in the body machine

Second, body joints have "oil" inside. Car engines and other machines have oil or grease, to make the parts move easily and last for years. This is called **lubrication**. The body's joints have their own slippery lubricating "oil", which is called **synovial fluid**. The bones and fluid are contained in a kind of bag called a **joint capsule**.

And third, joints have **ligaments**. These are like strong elastic bands around the joint, attached to the bones at each end. They work like "safety straps" to stop the bones moving too far and damaging the joint.

Joint designs

The body has different types of joints for different kinds of movements. These designs have various names.

	Joint	Movement	Examples
	Hinge	Back and forward only	Knee, elbow, smaller knuckles
	Ball-and socket	Lots of movement including twisting	Shoulder, hip
	Saddle	Back and forward, side-to-side	Base of the thumb
	Gliding	Limited sliding	Small bones of wrist, ankle
	Pivot	Turning or spinning so head can turn	Top of backbone under skull

lubrication   reducing wear and tear by using oil or a slippery substance
synovial fluid   slippery fluid that works like oil in a joint

Get a move on!

Joints, like muscles and bones, are designed to be used. If you laze about and don't take exercise, your joints begin to get stiff. They won't move so easily and smoothly. When you try to use them, they might ache or cause pain. To stop this problem getting worse, joints, muscles, and bones need regular exercise.

On guard!

If you try to do any fast–moving sports, wear protective guards over joints such as elbows, wrists, knees and ankles. These not only prevent skin scrapes and cuts. They also give extra protection to the joint, so it is less likely to get injured if you fall.

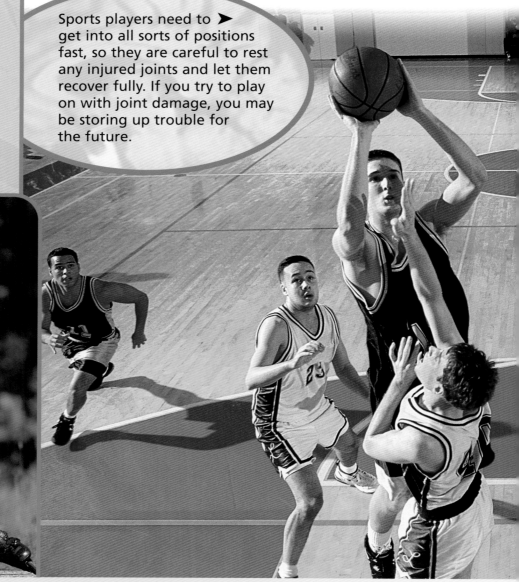

Sports players need to ➤ get into all sorts of positions fast, so they are careful to rest any injured joints and let them recover fully. If you try to play on with joint damage, you may be storing up trouble for the future.

disclocation   when bones in a joint move too far and come out of position
osteoarthritis   painful, stiff joints, usually due to worn-out cartilage

How much is too much?

Joints are designed to be used – but not too much. People who are very active for many years, especially athletes and sports players, take care not to over-use and sprain their joints. Otherwise, lots of small injuries happen, and gradually the damage increases. The smooth **cartilage** covering the bone ends in the joint becomes rough and flaky. This is known as **osteoarthritis** and brings on pain and stiffness.

When a joint "pops out"

Sometimes a joint cannot cope with the strain on it. This may happen in high-speed sports where people collide or fall. The bones slip or wrench apart, which is called a **dislocation** (shown below). This damages the joint and is very painful, but a doctor can move the bones back into their correct places.

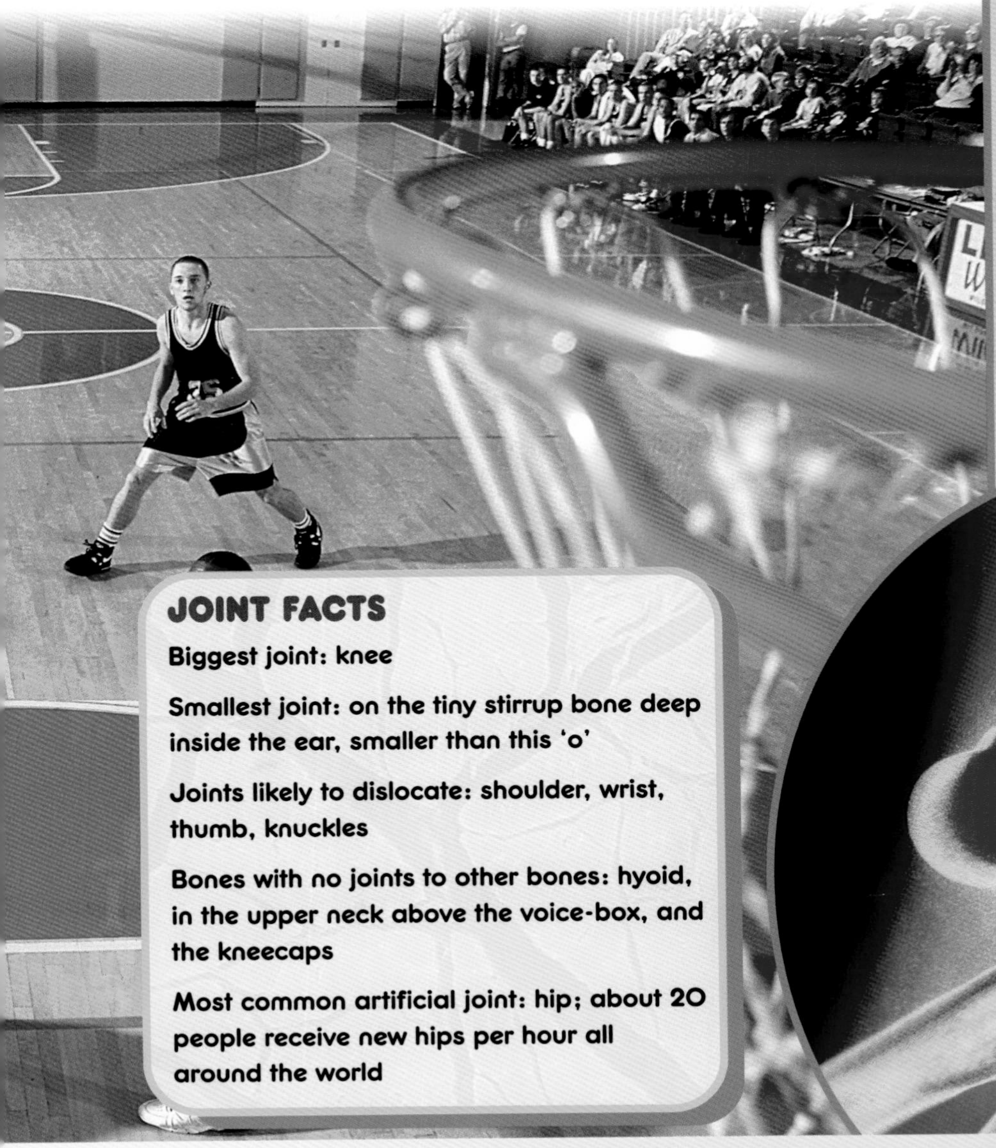

JOINT FACTS

Biggest joint: knee

Smallest joint: on the tiny stirrup bone deep inside the ear, smaller than this 'o'

Joints likely to dislocate: shoulder, wrist, thumb, knuckles

Bones with no joints to other bones: hyoid, in the upper neck above the voice-box, and the kneecaps

Most common artificial joint: hip; about 20 people receive new hips per hour all around the world

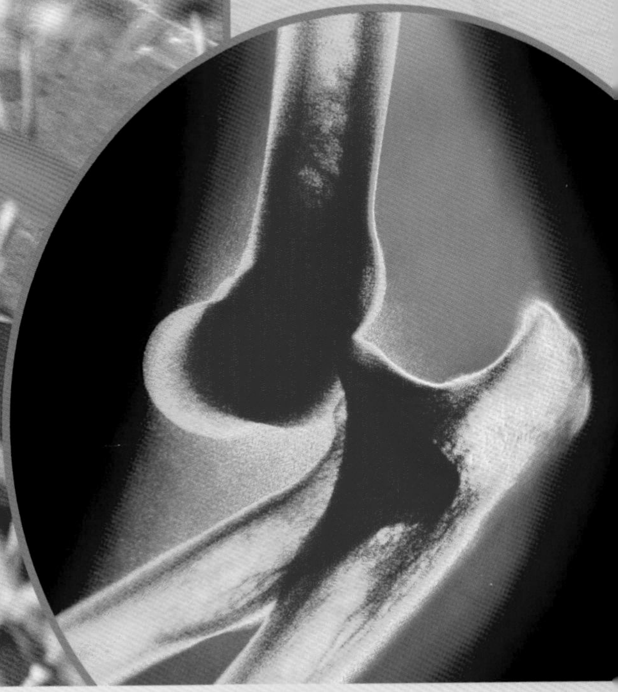

Muscling in

Muscles, muscles

The body's muscle system is complex. The picture below shows lots of them, and there is another set at the back. On the left side, the **superficial** muscles are shown, just under the skin. Beneath them is another set called intermediate muscles (shown on the right side). Under these is a third layer of muscles, right next to the skeleton.

Bones hold you up, but muscles make you move. Muscles are body parts with one simple task – to get shorter, or **contract**. They cause all your actions and movements, from pressing buttons on a mobile phone to leaping high in the air. And there are plenty of them. You have about 640 muscles, and they probably make up about two fifths of your total weight.

Most muscles are attached to bones at each end. When the muscle contracts, it pulls the bones closer together, which causes movement.

contract   become smaller or shorter, as when a muscle contracts and pulls on the bones attached to it

Biggest, smallest

Like bones, muscles are different shapes and sizes, depending on how powerful they need to be. The biggest are the gluteus maximus muscles, in your bottom. They pull the thigh bones backwards when you walk, run and jump. They are wide and slab-like, strong enough to lift the whole body into the air.

The stapedius muscle, deep inside the ear is tiny – hardly thicker than cotton thread. It pulls on the tiny stirrup bone when the ear hears very loud sounds. This protects the delicate hearing parts inside the ear.

◄ Muscles move the body into many different positions – and also keep it there. This diver's muscles lock his body in the same position for a second or two as he falls through the air.

Names, names

Every one of the 640 muscles in the body has a name. However only experts, like doctors, know all of them. Athletes, body-builders and sports players also know some names:

Delts   Deltoid, the large triangular-shaped muscle over each shoulder

Pecs   Pectoralis, the wide muscle at the front of the upper chest

Abs   Abdominals, the 'six-pack' muscles on the front of the lower body

Hamstrings   Muscles at the back of the thigh.

"Friday morning – gym. I focused on sit-ups and pull-ups because the coach says I need to tone my external obliques and abdominals, for a firmer belly."

Inside a muscle

Each muscle contains lots of rod-like fibres called myofibres, about as thick as hairs. Each of these contains many even smaller fibres, myofibrils. The muscle also has nerves to control its movement.

Team work

Unless you're asleep, you're using lots of your muscles most of the time. This is because muscles hardly ever work alone. They work as teams or groups. A simple action like turning over this page uses about 40 muscles in your hand and fingers. And that's not all. Your arm and shoulder muscles help to put your hand in the right place, as your back muscles tense to keep you balanced. Turning the page uses lots of muscles!

No push, only pull

Most muscles become narrower at each end, as a very strong, rope-like part called a **tendon**. The tendon is fixed firmly to the bone. When the muscle shortens, it pulls the tendon, which pulls the bone.

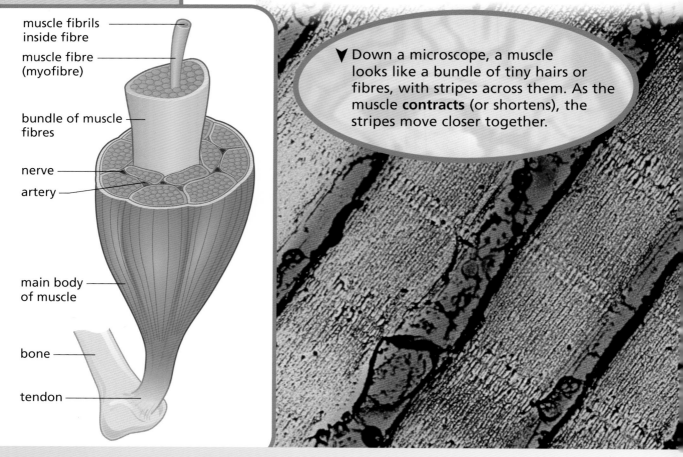

muscle fibrils inside fibre

muscle fibre (myofibre)

bundle of muscle fibres

nerve

artery

main body of muscle

bone

tendon

▼ Down a microscope, a muscle looks like a bundle of tiny hairs or fibres, with stripes across them. As the muscle **contracts** (or shortens), the stripes move closer together.

tendon   narrow end part of a muscle that joins to a bone

However, muscles can only pull. They can't make themselves longer and push. When you push something, like a lawnmower, there is actually a series of pulling movements in your muscles. In your shoulder, one set of muscles contracts to pulls your arm left. Another set of muscles pulls it to the right. Yet another set lifts your arm upwards. Meanwhile, the sets of muscles that aren't used relax and stretch out. Together, these pulling or relaxing muscles let you push forwards.

FIST AND WRIST

Curl your fingers into a fist and clench it hard. The main muscles that bend your fingers are not in the fingers themselves, but on the inside of your forearm. You can see them bulge as they pull hard. These muscles are connected to your fingers by long tendons that pass through your wrist. You might see these tendons tightening as you clench your fist.

Lots or bigger?

We say that people with well-developed muscles, like bodybuilders and weightlifters, have "lots of muscles". But they have the same number of muscles as anyone else – about 640. However, each muscle is bigger than normal, with more of the tiny fibres inside.

Smile away

It really is easier to smile than to frown. Smiling uses about 18 face muscles. Frowning uses over 40, which is more than twice as many. Making each muscle shorten uses energy. So save energy – smile your way through the day!

Turn that frown upside-down!

Your face and head contain more than 60 muscles that make facial expressions. With these expressions you can look surprised, angry, worried, happy, and sad, and show many other feelings – all without saying a word. Look in a mirror and practise some of these expressions. Can you see the muscles tightening under your skin?

Muscle-to-muscle

Some of your face muscles are not joined to bones at each end. They are joined to other muscles. As they **contract** and pull, they alter the shape of these other muscles. The other muscles can do the same and pull back. At each corner of your mouth, the ends of seven muscles come together at one place. As each one moves it affects the others. This is how your mouth can make so many shapes as it grins, smiles, frowns, sucks, and blows.

Making faces

◆ Raise one eyebrow only. That's the frontalis muscle tensing in your forehead.

◆ Grin widely. That's the risorius muscles pulling each side of your mouth.

◆ Sniff air in fast through your nose. That's the nasalis muscles making your nostrils wider.

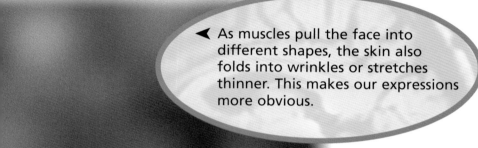

◄ As muscles pull the face into different shapes, the skin also folds into wrinkles or stretches thinner. This makes our expressions more obvious.

Bendiest muscle

Your tongue is almost entirely muscle. Look in a mirror as you pull in your tongue to the back of the mouth, making it wide and flat. Then poke it out, and it becomes long and thin. Some people can even curl it into a "U"!

Don't talk with your mouth full!

As you eat, don't speak. People don't want to see what you're chewing, and bits of food may dribble out! Talking and eating are two of our most common actions – although not at the same time. Like all movements, they are muscle-powered. Eating uses two main muscles on each side of the face. The **temporalis** goes from the side of the skull, above the ear, to the lower jaw. The **masseter** runs from the cheekbone to the lower jaw. Both pull up the lower jaw as you bite and chew.

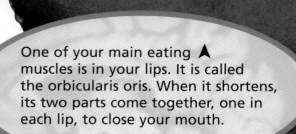

One of your main eating ▲ muscles is in your lips. It is called the orbicularis oris. When it shortens, its two parts come together, one in each lip, to close your mouth.

masseter   strong muscle between the cheekbone and lower jaw
temporalis   strong muscle between the side of the head and lower jaw

It's all talk

To speak, you use about 40 muscles in your chest, neck, **voicebox**, throat, and mouth. The chest muscles push air up from your lungs, through your voicebox. The faster the air flows, the louder you talk. Voicebox muscles alter the shape of the voicebox to make high or low sounds. Your face, tongue and lip muscles change the shape of your mouth, so you can say words clearly. If you try to speak without moving your lips or tongue, you won't make much sense!

FEEL LIKE A BITE?

Pretend to chew gum and touch your head above your ear. You can feel the temporalis muscle bulge. Also, feel the masseter muscle bulge between your cheekbone and jaw.

Blink, wink

Your two busiest face muscles work perhaps 30,000 times each day. They are called orbicularis oculi – better known as the eyelids. Each of these muscles has two parts – the upper and lower eyelids. When they shorten, they close the gap between them, and you blink (both eyes) or wink (one eye only).

Day by day

Exercise doesn't have to be organized in a special place with special equipment. We can do it every day, like walking or cycling instead of sitting in the car. Some of the best forms of all-over exercise include swimming and dancing.

Go for it – every day

What kind of exercise suits you best? Walking? Cycling? Swimming? Like bones and joints, muscles are designed to be used. The more you move around, carry out activities and play sports, then the healthier you become.

If muscles aren't used regularly, they become floppy and weak and waste away. They cannot tense to hold body parts steady, and they are not strong enough to pull hard. This increases the risk of muscle strains, joint **sprains**, accidents and injuries.

When you rest

Muscles power your heartbeat and breathing, and these benefit from exercise too. When you rest, only a little blood flows to your relaxed muscles – about one litre each minute. You breathe about seven litres of air in and out per minute.

When you're active

However when you're very active, like running, the amount of blood to your muscles rises to more than 10 litres each minute. So your heart has to pump harder and faster to supply this blood. Also you breathe harder and faster, more than 50 litres of air each minute. This extra work helps to keep your heart and lungs healthy, as well as your muscles.

Using muscles is not just healthy. ➤ Exercise and sport give many people a 'buzz' and make them feel much better and happier – especially when they do well!

cramp   when a muscle contracts hard and painfully, out of control

OUCH! OW! THAT HURTS!

Muscles which are not very strong and healthy may be unable to cope when they are suddenly used. They might suddenly become very hard, tense and tight, and you cannot relax them. This is called cramp, and it hurts! If you get it, gently stretch and rub or massage the muscle for a few minutes.

Warm up, cool down

Athletes and sports people know the importance of warm-up exercises before an event, and cool-down ones afterwards. These get the muscles warm and flexible and the joints moving. Otherwise sudden jerks and wrenching may cause injury.

Let's work together

Jumping high

High-jumping uses the largest muscles in the body, the gluteus maximus in your bottom. This pulls the thigh back, to thrust the body upwards. Other powerful muscles straighten the knee joint and tilt the foot for the best power at take-off.

Bones give the body support and protection. Joints let the bones move easily. Muscles provide the power for movement. These three **body systems** work together all the time as we walk, talk, run, eat, stand, push, lean, lift, and carry out hundreds more actions every day. For example, imagine you're walking past some people throwing and catching a ball. Suddenly one of the throws goes wrong, and the ball aims straight for your head!

body system   various parts that work together to carry out one main task
stamina   ability to carry out movements for a long time, without fatigue

Look out!

At once you use your muscles, bones and joints. You probably close your eyes and screw up your face, tensing the muscles there. You may bring up your hand in front of your face for protection, using your shoulder and arm muscles and joints. Your hand and finger bones are held out like a shield. Your neck muscles turn your head away from the ball. Your back muscles bend your back, so you lean to one side, out of the way. Meanwhile your leg muscles work fast so you keep your balance. All this happens in a second, and saves you from injury.

▼ A simple ball-throwing action uses more than 30 bones, 50 joints and 100 muscles in the shoulder, arm, hand and fingers. The arm flicks out straight in front, and the fingers release the ball at exactly the right moment.

Big isn't always best

Many top athletes and sports stars don't have huge, bulging muscles. Champions need lots of other features as well. They need to learn the right techniques, and build up **stamina** to use muscles for a long time. Of course, they also need the drive or motivation to get better and better.

Nerve into muscle

Nerve messages travel in the form of tiny electrical signals, called nerve impulses. The nerve joins to the muscle at many tiny, spider-shaped parts called **motor end plates**. These spread the signals throughout the muscle, so that the many tiny muscle fibres **contract** together.

All under control

When you finish reading, you might close this book and move around. But before that, think about how you will make these movements.

You will use your bones, muscles and joints – and your brain. Your brain controls your muscles. It tells them when to contract, by how much, and for how long. It does this by sending messages to the muscles along **nerves**.

As we carry out delicate movements, ➤ we watch them carefully. If the movement is not quite right, we can adjust the muscles to correct it, again and again as we continue. This is called hand-eye coordination.

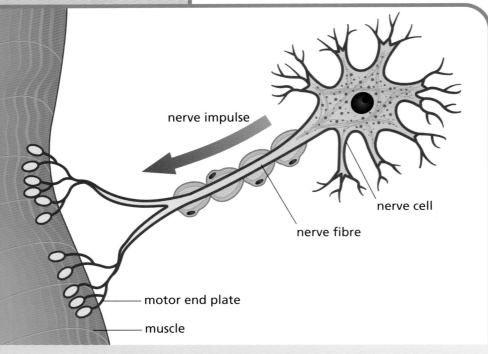

nerve impulse

nerve cell

nerve fibre

motor end plate

muscle

cerebellum   part at the brain's rear that coordinates muscle actions to make movements skilful

In the brain

The message to move begins in an area on the top of your brain called the **motor centre**. This is where you decide to carry out an action. It starts as a general message, "lift hand". This goes from the motor centre to a lower part of the brain called the **cerebellum**. This works out the details of the movement and sends hundreds of messages to dozens of muscles in your shoulder, arm and hand. The cerebellum makes sure the muscles all work together to make your action smooth and easy, rather than jerky and clumsy.

Movement control

Your brain's motor centre is where you make the main decision to carry out an action. It is a strap-shaped region across the top of the brain. The cerebellum organizes the movement in more detail. It is the bulging, wrinkled part at the lower rear of the brain. Messages then go out along nerves to the muscles.

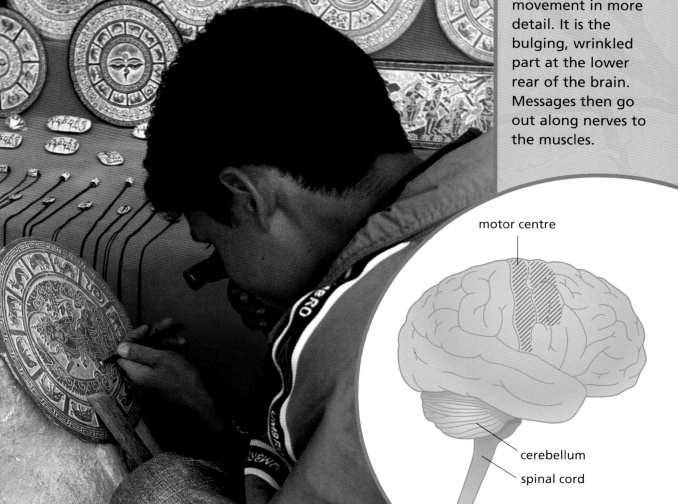

motor centre

cerebellum

spinal cord

motor centre   strap-shaped region on the brain's cerebral cortex, which controls muscle movement
motor end plates   where nerve fibres join muscle and pass signals to make them shorten

Auto-muscles

All of the muscles mentioned so far in this book are called skeletal muscles, because most of them join to bones of the skeleton. They can also be called striped muscles, because they have a pattern of very tiny bands or stripes. A third name for them is **voluntary** muscles, because they work when you decide, or volunteer, to make a movement. However these muscles are not the only ones in your body. There are two other types.

What involuntary muscles do

✦ **Gullet** – squeeze food down to the stomach
✦ **Stomach** – mash food for digestion
✦ **Guts** – push food along to take its goodness into the body
✦ **End of guts** – hold in waste until you can use the toilet
✦ **Ureters** – tubes that squeeze urine from the kidneys to the bladder
✦ **Bladder** – hold in urine until you can use the toilet

When you sleep, most of your ▼ skeletal muscles are relaxed and floppy. But inside the body you are on autopilot! Your involuntary auto-muscles are at work, helping to digest food and get body wastes ready for removal.

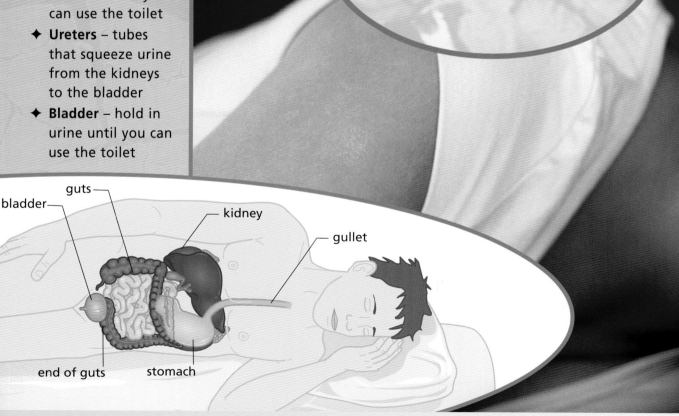

bladder — guts — kidney — gullet — end of guts — stomach

viscera   soft parts such as stomach, intestines, liver, and pancreas
voluntary   muscles which work when we want them to, not automatically

Muscles inside

The second kind of muscle is called visceral muscle. This is because it is found in the **viscera** – the soft parts inside the main body, like your stomach and guts. This muscle forms layers in the walls of these parts. It squashes food in the stomach and squeezes it through the guts. It is also called smooth muscle, because it doesn't have tiny stripes like the skeletal muscles. It is called involuntary muscle because it works automatically. You don't have to think about it, or "order" it to work.

Auto-problems

Involuntary muscles are controlled by parts of the brain. But we are not aware of this control and we hardly ever notice these auto-muscles working – until they don't. If a person suffers brain injury, the auto-control areas may be affected. This can cause problems such as urinary incontinence, when the person cannot keep in urine.

AUTO-MUSCLE POWER

It takes about 24 hours for one meal to be swallowed, go through your digestive system and out as waste. This takes a lot of auto-muscle power!

A very special muscle

Your whole body depends on a "bag of muscle" which works non-stop through life. It is the special, third type of muscle, which keeps your whole body alive, every second of every day. This is the **cardiac** muscle. Thick layers of it make up the walls of your heart. When the heart muscle contracts, it squeezes the blood inside the heart out into **blood vessels** called **arteries**, and all around the body. When the heart muscle relaxes, blood flows into the heart from the **blood vessels** called **veins**. One squeeze-and-relax action is called a heartbeat.

Hollow heart

A cutaway view of the heart shows its walls, which are almost all muscle. This heart muscle is thickest in the lower parts or chambers of the heart, called **ventricles**. These provide most of the pumping power.

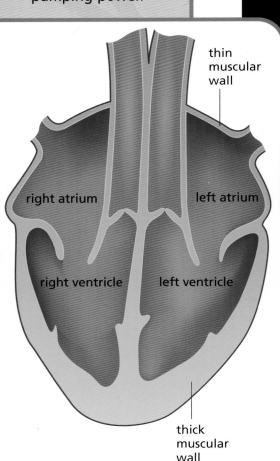

thin muscular wall

right atrium

left atrium

right ventricle

left ventricle

thick muscular wall

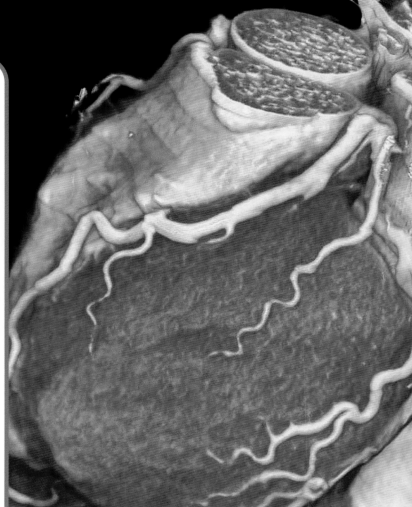

coronary arteries   blood vessels which carry blood to the heart muscle
cardiac   to do with the heart

Never tired

In most people the heart beats slightly more than once per second. That's more than 2,500 million beats in an average lifetime. Luckily, heart muscle is different from skeletal muscle. It never gets tired, or **fatigued**. But, just like other muscles, it needs a good supply of blood to bring the energy to work. This blood comes along small blood vessels called **coronary arteries**, which branch and divide into the heart muscle.

Muscles and machines	watts (units of power)
Laser-pen pointer	0.002
Human heart	2
Human body running fast	100
Family car on the motorway	100,000
Space shuttle	10,000 million

Spiky lines

All muscles give out tiny amounts or "waves" of electricity when they work. **Sensor** pads, placed on the chest or other parts of the body, can detect the electricity from the heart's muscle. The "waves" are shown on a screen or paper strip as a spiky line called an ECG (electro cardiogram). Unusual shapes in the line may be a sign of heart trouble.

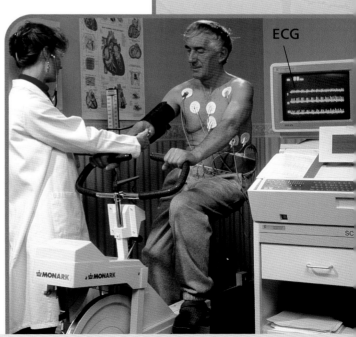

ECG

◄ The heart is really just a hollow bag with thick walls made of cardiac muscle. The snake–like coronary arteries branch over its surface.

sensor part which detects something, like light, sound or the level of a substance inside itself, and sends messages to the brain
ventricles two lower pumping chambers of the heart

Find out more

Quiz answers

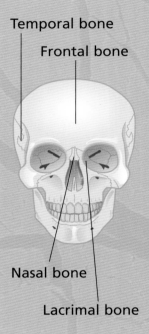

Temporal bone

Frontal bone

Nasal bone

Lacrimal bone

Books

Muscles: Injury, Illnes and Health, Carol Ballard (Heinemann Library, 2003)

Heart and Blood, Injury, Illness and Health, Carol Ballard (Heinemann Library, 2003)

Are you tough enough?, Paul Mason, (Raintree, 2005)

Training for the top, Paul Mason, (Raintree, 2005)

World Wide Web

If you want to find out more about muscles and bones, you can search the Internet using keywords like these:

- 'striated muscle'
- diet + fitness
- bone marrow

You can also find your own keywords by using headings or words from this book. Use the search tips opposve to help you find the most useful websites.

COMMON KNOWLEDGE?

The body's biggest tendon is the calcaneal tendon. It joins the calf muscle to the heel bone, or calcaneus. But it has a more common name; the Achilles tendon. Can you find out why it is called this?

Search tips

There are billions of pages on the Internet so it can be difficult to find exactly what you are looking for. For example, if you just type in 'water' on a search engine like Google, you will get a list of 19 million web pages. These search skills will help you find useful websites more quickly:

- Use simple keywords instead of whole sentences
- Use two to six keywords in a search, putting the most important words first
- Be precise – only use names of people, places or things
- If you want to find words that go together, put quote marks around them, for example 'stomach acid' or 'length of intestine'
- Use the advanced section of your search engine
- Use the + sign between keywords to link them, for example typing + KS3 after your keyword will help you find web pages at the right level.

Where to search

Search engine

A search engine looks through the entire web and lists all sites that match the words in the search box. It can give thousands of links, but the best matches are at the top of the list, on the first page. Try **bbc.co.uk/search**

Search directory

A search directory is like a library of websites that have been sorted by a person instead of a computer. You can search by keyword or subject and browse through the different sites like you look through books on a library shelf. A good example is **yahooligans.com**

Glossary

arteries larger blood vessels that carry blood away from the heart

blood vessel arteries, capillaries and veins, through which blood flows

body system various parts that work together to carry out one main task

bone marrow jelly-like substance inside certain bones, which makes new blood cells and stores nutrients

cardiac to do with the heart

cartilage tough, springy substance, sometimes called "gristle", that covers the ends of bones inside a joint, and forms some parts of the skeleton

cells microscopic "building blocks" which make up all body parts

cerebellum part at the brain's rear that coordinates muscle actions to make movements skilfull

collagen tough, string-like fibres found in body parts such as the skin and bones

contract become smaller or shorter, as when a muscle contracts and pulls on the bones attached to it

coronary arteries blood vessels which carry blood to the heart muscle

cramp when a muscle contracts hard and painfully, out of control

cranium domed upper part of the skull

dislocation when the bones in a joint move too far and come out of position

fontanelle gaps between the skull bones of a young baby, which eventually closes

fracture break or crack

fuse join very strongly, so hardly any joint remains

joint capsule bag-like part around bone ends in a joint, containing synovial fluid

lever crowbar-like, able to move heavy loads

ligament "strap" that holds bones together at a joint and stops them moving too far

lubrication reducing wear and tear by using oil or a slippery substance

masseter strong muscle between the cheekbone and lower jaw

meninges three thin layers that nourish and protect the brain and spinal cord,

minerals substances, such as iron, the body needs to stay healthy

motor centre strap-shaped region on brain's cerebral cortex, which controls muscle movement

motor end plate where nerve fibres join muscle fibres and pass signals to make them shorten

nerves string-like parts that carry messages around the body as tiny pulses of electricity

nutrients substances in food that the body needs to be healthy, grow and heal

osteoarthritis painful, stiff joints, usually due to worn-out cartilage

oxygen gas, which makes up one-fifth of air, that each body cell needs

red blood cells cells specialized to carry oxygen around the body

sensor part which detects something, like light, sound or the level of a certain substance inside itself, and sends messages to the brain

skull main bone inside the head, which is really more than 20 separate bones joined firmly together.

spinal cord main nerve linking the brain to the rest of the body

sprain when a joint is forced to move too far, damaging the soft parts

stamina ability to carry out movements for a long time, without fatigue

stem cells cells that make specialized cells such as skin or blood cells

superficial on or near the surface

sutures fixed joints, where bones have joined solidly together

synovial fluid slippery fluid that works like oil in a joint

temporalis strong muscle between the side of the head and lower jaw

tendon narrow end part of a muscle that joins to a bone

vein large blood vessel that carries blood to the heart

ventricles two lower pumping chambers of the heart

vertebrae individual bones of the backbone, which join like links in a chain

viscera soft parts, such as the stomach, intestines, liver, and pancreas.

voicebox also called the larynx, this part makes sounds as we speak, hum, cry and make other noises

voluntary muscles that work when we want them to, not automatically

Index

Titles in the *Body Talk* series include:

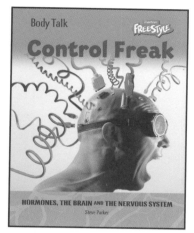

Hardback   1 4062 0062 X

Hardback   1 4062 0061 1

Hardback   1 4062 0065 4

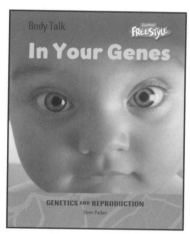

Hardback   1 4062 0063 8

Hardback   1 4062 0066 2

Hardback   1 4062 0064 6

Find out about the other titles in this series on our website www.raintreepublishers.co.uk